Erie Maritime Museum
and U.S. Brig Niagara

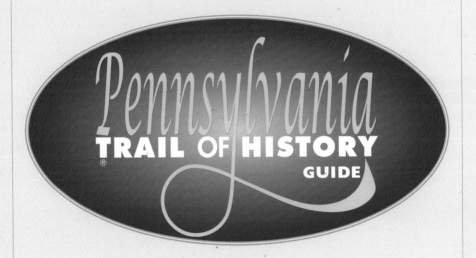

Text by Chris J. Magoc

STACKPOLE
BOOKS

PENNSYLVANIA HISTORICAL
AND MUSEUM COMMISSION

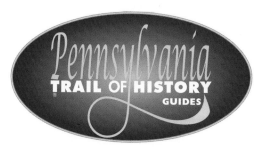

Kyle R. Weaver, Series Editor
Tracy Patterson, Designer

Published by
STACKPOLE BOOKS
5067 Ritter Road
Mechanicsburg, Pennsylvania 17055

Pennsylvania Trail of History® is a registered trademark of the Pennsylvania Historical and Museum Commission.

Printed in the United States of America
10 9 8 7 6 5 4 3 2 1
FIRST EDITION

Maps by Caroline Stover

Photography
Art Becker Photography: cover, 5
Lowry Photography: 3
All other credits are noted throughout

Library of Congress Cataloging-in-Publication Data

Magoc, Chris J., 1960–
    Erie Maritime Museum and U.S. brig Niagara / text by Chris J. Magoc—1st ed.
        p. cm.—(Pennsylvania trail of history guides)
    Includes bibliographical references.
    ISBN 0-8117-2756-4
    1. Erie, Lake, Battle of, 1813. 2. Niagara (Brig) 3. Erie Maritime Museum—Guidebooks. 4. Erie (Pa.)—History, Naval. 5. Erie, Lake, Region—History, Naval. 6. Pennsylvania—History—War of 1812—Naval operations. 7. United States—History—War of 1812—Naval operations. I. Title. II. Series.

E356.E6 M23 2001
973.5'23—dc21

00-047000

Contents

Editor's Preface

The Pennsylvania Trail of History Guides is a series of handbooks on the historic sites and museums administered by the Pennsylvania Historical and Museum Commission (PHMC). Stackpole Books is proud to continue the project with this volume.

The series was conceived and created by Stackpole Books with the cooperation of the PHMC's Division of Publications and Bureau of Historic Sites and Museums. The latter is headed by Donna Williams, and she and the bureau staff have contributed their considerable expertise to the project through many useful memos and meetings. Diane Reed, Chief of Publications, has facilitated relations between the PHMC and Stackpole from the project's inception, organized the review process with the commission, and attended to numerous details related to the venture.

For this volume, Robert Johnson, Administrator of Erie Maritime Museum, and Capt. Walter Rybka, Master of the U.S. Brig *Niagara*, have been cooperative in meeting our needs during the research and editorial stages of this volume. Richard Liebel, Public Relations Director for the museum, coordinated meetings and provided assistance in gathering photographs of the museum exhibits and the ship.

Chris J. Magoc, the author of the text, has degrees in American studies from Pennsylvania State University (M.A.) and University of New Mexico (Ph.D.) and is currently a professor of American history at Mercyhurst College in Erie. He was formerly Director of Education at Erie Maritime Museum and was responsible for developing the interpretive plan for the museum and the *Niagara*. That background is evident here in his recounting of Erie's maritime history, from the crucial Battle of Lake Erie in 1813 to the city's rich fishing heritage; his telling of the post-battle story of *Niagara*, its scuttling and raising, reconstruction and decay, and recent rebirth; and his armchair tour of the museum and ship.

Kyle R. Weaver, Editor
Stackpole Books

Introduction to the Site

E rie Maritime Museum serves as home port for the U.S. Brig
Niagara, a historically accurate reconstruction of the relief flagship used by Commodore Oliver Hazard Perry in the Battle of
Lake Erie during the War of 1812. Dedicated in 1990 as the flagship of
Pennsylvania, *Niagara* maintains an active sailing program, voyaging
to ports throughout the Great Lakes and along the Atlantic coast.
Whether sailing or in home port, the ship's crew and docents tell the
dramatic story of the pivotal role the original ship played in the September 10, 1813, battle that regained control of the Old Northwest
region for the United States during its war against Great Britain.

Through exhibits and programs, Erie Maritime Museum illustrates
the battle and the war, as well as the central themes of Erie's post-1813
naval and maritime history, including the story of the USS
Michigan/Wolverine, the U.S. Navy's first iron-hulled warship; Erie's
status as the world's leading freshwater fishing port in the early twentieth century; and the environmental degradation and rebirth of Lake
Erie. Administered by the Pennsylvania Historical and Museum Commission, the museum and ship are supported by the Flagship Niagara
League, which provides volunteers, staff, and funds, and also maintains
the museum's gift shop, the Shipwright Shop.

The Battle of Lake Erie and Erie's Maritime Heritage

T he bloody conflict that made *Niagara* legendary was, in fact, just one relatively small engagement in a series of world wars, and it is in that larger context that the War of 1812 and Battle of Lake Erie are best understood. In the spring of 1812 Great Britain and France, Europe's great imperial powers, had been at war almost continuously since 1793. Throughout the nearly twenty-year Napoleonic Wars, the fledgling United States maintained an official position of neutrality, while trying to continue trading with both warring powers. England and France were each intent on preventing American trade with its enemy, thus setting the stage for inevitable conflict.

With the most powerful navy the world had ever seen, the British were in a much stronger position than the French to interfere with American commerce. British naval vessels occasionally seized American merchant ships and, more routinely, impressed into service in the Royal Navy thousands of sailors from U.S. ships (estimates range between five and seven thousand). Many of these men were deserters from the Royal Navy;

many more claimed American citizenship. To the British, desperately short of sailors to man their fleet, it mattered little. For nearly a decade, British impressment of American sailors and interference with American trade provoked cries at home of "free trade, sailors' rights." Trade sanctions imposed by the administration of President Thomas Jefferson generally backfired, only increasing the sense of frustration. For some Americans, British actions constituted a serious threat to the young nation's honor and made military confrontation increasingly seem the only choice.

Yet in the early nineteenth century, Americans were not closely bound together economically or politically. Relatively few citizens in the interior of the country wished to rush to war over the issue of maritime rights. But what Americans in the southern and western portions of the country did feel was the urge to expand, and that issue became pivotal in the decision to go to war. By 1812 Americans had pushed their frontier into the Ohio River valley. Some had crossed into British-controlled Canada. The

The Victory on Lake Erie boosted national morale and made Oliver Hazard Perry a hero.

U.S. NAVAL ACADEMY MUSEUM

Impressment of the American Sailor. *Illustrator Howard Pyle (1853–1911) depicted the practice of British warship commanders who seized American merchant ships and drafted sailors into the Royal Navy. Thousands of those impressed were naturalized Americans, and this disregard for their rights contributed to the growing sentiment to restore American honor by going to war.* U.S. NAVAL ACADEMY MUSEUM

British perceived American westward expansion as a threat to their hold on the lucrative fur trade in the northern wilderness. With hopes of checking the Americans, the British began supplying arms to a confederation of Indian tribes that had united under the leadership of the great Shawnee chief Tecumseh.

The remarkable pan-tribal confederation that extended from the Great Lakes all the way to the Gulf coast had been brought together by Tecumseh and his brother, Tenskwatawa, "The Prophet." Indian tribes resisted American invasion of their sacred homelands and traditional hunting grounds. Having lost nearly five million acres of land between 1795 and 1809, natives were determined to halt the advance of the Americans in the Ohio and Mississippi River valleys. The ideology of white Americans, later labeled Manifest Destiny, held that divine providence had ordained the continent, including British Canada, to be theirs for the taking. The natives, supplied by the British who feared an Ameri-

can invasion of Canada, began attacking and raiding white settlements along the frontier, particularly after the Indian defeat at the Battle of Tippecanoe in November 1811. Most American frontiersmen feared and loathed Indians, and the native-British alliance, though purely one of military and strategic necessity, only increased their hostility toward the nation they had defeated only a generation before in the Revolution.

Cries for war in 1812 were loudest from a group of Republican congressmen in the South and West who became known as the "war hawks." Kentuckian Henry Clay spoke loudly for his constituents, who wanted to be rid of both the British and the Indians. By contrast, New England states, heavily dependent on British trade, vigorously opposed the call to war, for as strained as the maritime economy was, things obviously would get a lot worse if war was declared. As indeed it was, albeit by a precariously close vote. The June 17, 1812, vote carried the U.S. House of

Representatives by a margin of only 79 to 49, and the Senate by 19 to 13. Most prowar votes were southern and western, and Republican—the party of Jefferson and President James Madison—in political affiliation; those opposed were largely from the Northeast and aligned with the Federalist party, which had long resisted western expansionism. (Pennsylvania's congressional delegation, dominated by Republicans, voted 18-2 in favor of war.)

It is possible that this close vote would have gone the other way, if communications had been better in 1812. In the third week of June, Great Britain rescinded her Orders in Council, a set of restrictive policies that cut off maritime trade between the United States and northern Europe. Very damaging to British commercial interests, the Orders in Council had also provoked the wrath of American merchants. Word that the Orders in Council had been rescinded would surely have altered the politics of the war debate, but news of the action arrived in Washington days after the declaration of war.

WAR IN THE NORTHWEST

The United States entered the War of 1812 spectacularly unprepared. Against Great Britain's Royal Navy of nearly 700 vessels, Americans boasted a grand total of 17 warships in commission. Some American leaders believed the declaration of war would bluff the British into ceasing their interference with American ships and westward expansion and that actual combat would prove unnecessary. Why indeed would the British want to divert men and ships to North America from the overwhelmingly more pressing cause of defeating Napoleon in Europe?

Other American leaders held that should matters lead to war, the conflict could be won on land. Former President Jefferson was among those who believed that the invasion and taking of Canada from the British—the chief U.S. military objective in the war—would be a "mere matter of marching" and that the American naval disadvantage could therefore be overcome. Events proved otherwise. Indeed, one of the many great ironies of the war is that Americans generally fared better on the sea than on land, where things ground to a bloody stalemate. The U.S. Navy successfully cut its teeth in several victories by the USS *Constitution* and other frigates on the open sea, as well as at the Battle of Lake Erie and the Battle of Lake Champlain. On land, however, British troops and their Indian allies quickly gained the upper hand

President James Madison. The genius of American political theory faced the test of putting his ideas into practice during his term as chief executive. EDITOR'S COLLECTION

9

during the summer of 1812. After a failed attempt by the United States to invade Canada, the British retaliated and captured the American forts of Dearborn (Chicago), Mackinac, and Detroit. By the fall, all of Michigan Territory lay in their hands, and all of the Northwest Territory appeared vulnerable.

BUILDING AND MANNING THE LAKE ERIE FLEET

For both sides, military control of the Great Lakes, particularly Erie and Ontario, meant continued supplies of men and materials to the frontier outposts, which in turn determined control of the war in the Northwest. Because of Niagara Falls and the Lachine Rapids at Montreal, oceangoing ships of the Royal Navy could not be brought in to Lake Erie to defend what was called Upper Canada—the region *up* the St. Lawrence River. Although they started out with some warships, clearly the British would have to construct and outfit additional ships on Lake Erie. And with sparse manufacturing capacity in Canada and their supply lines running all the way to England, that would prove to be a particularly difficult challenge for the British.

For the Americans, retaking hold of western Lake Erie and the frontier rested on exploiting that one key advantage: the relative proximity of materials, manufacturing facilities, and skilled labor— the essential elements with which they could construct a fleet of well-armed ships that could overpower the British in one key battle.

Organizing that task fell to Daniel Dobbins, an Erie shipmaster who unwittingly found himself in the middle of the war in the Northwest. Dobbins happened to be selling salt at Fort Mackinac when the fort was taken by the British in the late summer of 1812. After losing his ship, Dobbins was paroled and made his way back to Erie and eventually to Washington, D.C., where he conveyed the grim news to President James Madison that the Northwest frontier was in enemy hands. It soon became apparent that the British threat could be reversed in a single naval action with a fleet of well-armed ships. Dobbins successfully argued to the president that the place to construct those vessels was the frontier village of Erie. Erie was an ideal site because Presque Isle—a long spit of sand jutting out along the mainland— offered a sheltered harbor within which a shipyard was reasonably invulnerable to attack.

With the initial sum of $2,000 (the entire squadron eventually cost $230,000), winter coming on, and this enormous task in front of him, Dobbins returned to Erie. Because a British attack seemed a very real possibility once spring arrived, Dobbins could not wait. He began the massive task of ordering supplies. By late winter, materials and men were arriving in great quantity: tons of shot and anchors and miles of rigging from Pittsburgh, thousands of square feet of sailcloth from Philadelphia, dozens of cannons from Washington, D.C., and New Jersey. A couple hundred shipbuilders had to come from the eastern seaboard, for Erie was a town of fewer than five hundred, with few skilled in the maritime trades. And buildings had to be constructed to house the men, for there were few if any accommodations for the influx of laborers. Everything but the timber, it seemed, came over the mountains on roads and trails that barely existed. Most of the materials arrived via Pittsburgh up the Allegheny River to French Creek—even as they were beginning to freeze that winter— and then overland from Waterford the

Oliver Hazard Perry. *The young master commandant from Rhode Island arrived in Erie in early 1813 to oversee the shipyard, raise a crew, and lead the American fleet.*
U.S. NAVAL ACADEMY MUSEUM

last twenty miles. For this reason, the naval war on the lakes, and the Battle of Lake Erie in particular, has often been called a "shipwright's war." It can be argued that the battle really was won during the winter and spring of 1812–13 with the building and manning of the Lake Erie fleet.

In January 1813, Commodore Isaac Chauncey arrived from Lake Ontario to inspect the shipyard. Concerned about the small size of four of the gunboats, he ordered two of them to be lengthened. One month later, he wrote to Noah Brown, a seasoned shipbuilder from New York, and ordered two large, twenty-gun brigs. Brown's arrival in Erie accelerated the pace of the work. Efficiency, not beauty or longevity, was the first goal of the shipbuilders. As Brown put it: "Though staunchly built, we want no extras. Plain work is all that is required; they will be wanted for only one battle. If we win that is all that is wanted of them. If the enemy is victorious, the work is good enough to be captured."

Desperately seeking a command, Master Commandant Oliver Hazard

Perry arrived from Rhode Island in March of 1813 to assume command of the vessels. Perry had been languishing in frustration through the early stage of the war and had requested to be transferred to the Great Lakes fleets under the command of Chauncey. Perry faced great challenges upon his arrival, not least among them the recruitment of several hundred sailors that could win the upcoming battle.

The U.S. Navy was strictly volunteer and haphazard in overall administration during the War of 1812. It fell to a commander to recruit his own men. Perry brought nearly one hundred sailors with him from Rhode Island, while other skilled seamen arrived from Chauncey's fleet on Lake Ontario. The majority of Perry's crew, however, came from the ranks of "landsmen"—regular army, marine, and militia units from Pennsylvania, Ohio, and Kentucky. For the most part, these were ill-trained soldiers and frontiersmen, some persuaded to fight by the lure of "prize money"—the share of money traditionally awarded to crew members in a naval battle from the sale of captured enemy ships.

Perry's frustration with Chauncey, his superior, over the numbers and quality of men he was sent resulted at one point that summer in his resignation from command, quickly withdrawn. Nevertheless, by the middle of the summer, Perry had amalgamated from these various sources a crew of approximately 400 men—though he had wanted 700 or more—of whom about 200 were experienced seamen who knew their way around a warship. An additional 100 soldiers came from the army of General William Henry Harrison in August. Perry and his officers spent the better part of the summer drilling the crew into an effective fighting force, a task made more difficult by the onset of a variety of diseases: measles, malaria, typhus, influenza, and an assortment of maladies known vaguely as "ague" or "lake fever," the latter likely caused by a combination of poor sanitation, malnutrition, and drinking lake water. On any given day that summer, one out of four of Perry's men was too ill to report for duty.

Earlier that spring, British commander Robert Barclay had faced a more dire situation on the western end of the lake at Amherstburg: fewer ships, poorly outfitted with cannons taken from the battery armament at Fort Malden; a crew about the same size as Perry's but with far fewer sailors; 14,000 Indian allies encamped nearby, increasingly eager to fight and drawing heavily on his food supplies. By late summer, Barclay was feeding his own men half rations and was reduced to several days' store of flour. In order to get resupplied, he would have to sail east, which would mean engaging Perry's fleet.

For Perry, a major obstacle lay in getting the fleet out into the lake. One of the chief advantages of the Presque Isle harbor was the sandbar that extended from the tip of Presque Isle; above that spit of sand was only six feet of water, at best. This served well for keeping the British ships at bay all summer, but now the American vessels had to get over that bar. Even with the two large brigs built with a shallow, nine-foot draft, there were still three or four feet of sand over which the three-hundred-ton ships had to be lifted. Noah Brown's answer to the dilemma was an ancient process called *cameling*, whereby the men constructed four long, shallow barges, or camels, equipped with hand pumps and holes in their bottoms that could be plugged. One brig at a time was off-loaded and partially rigged down, and then the camels were placed alongside and attached to the ship with timbers, two on either side. The camels were submerged by half filling them with water. Then, with crewmen pumping out the water from the camels, the ships were lifted just enough for men up ahead in a smaller boat to kedge the ship forward using the ship's capstan. The laborious process was repeated several times for each ship.

In May, Barclay sailed toward the eastern end of the lake and established his headquarters at Long Point, Ontario. On June 25, he began a naval blockade of the harbor but felt ill prepared to mount an attack from such a position, with the harbor seemingly well defended with militia. Perry seized the opportunity to camel the ships when, inexplicably, on July 31, Barclay pulled his ships away from Erie to sail back across the lake. Once over the bar, Perry ordered the ships quickly rearmed and sailed north, then west, to meet the enemy. For the remainder of August, Perry's fleet of ten ships cruised western Lake Erie. By early September, he had anchored among the Bass Islands in Put-in-Bay, located 140 miles west of Erie, near present-day Sandusky, Ohio, just off the far southwestern shores of the lake. There he waited for Barclay, who, though not fully prepared, became increasingly desperate to get resupplied.

THE BATTLE

At dawn on September 10, 1813, Perry spotted Barclay's fleet to the northwest of Put-in-Bay. He quickly weighed anchor and made ready to sail. Initially that morning, the wind had been blowing against Perry, and he had to tack back and forth in order to move toward Barclay. Perry had given each of the nine vessel commanders instructions as to the line of battle: The two brigs, *Lawrence* and *Niagara*, were to face the two British ships, *Queen Charlotte* and *Detroit*, while

AFRICAN AMERICANS IN THE BATTLE OF LAKE ERIE

One of the most vital components of Commodore Perry's crew during the Battle of Lake Erie was a contingent of well-seasoned African American sailors. Most of these men had seen previous service on other naval vessels, some having fought aboard the USS *Constitution* in earlier battles during the war.

Although racism and prejudice certainly existed, seafaring was one of the few jobs a black man could get in the early nineteenth century and be accorded relative equity in

pay and overall treatment. In one of his harangues to Commander Chauncey, Perry complained of having been sent "a motley set—Negroes, soldiers and boys." This quote is often taken out of the context of his larger frustration with recruitment, for Perry certainly had nothing but high praise for the African American seamen. He particularly noted their apparent fearlessness. Chauncey himself counted the black sailors in his fleet as being "amongst my best men."

the smaller vessels would battle ships of their own class. Dobbins's *Ohio* had left, ordered by Perry back to Erie for supplies. (One of Dobbins's great lifelong regrets was having missed the battle.) The U.S. fleet, therefore, numbered nine ships to the British six. The total number of guns was about equal, but Perry's squadron had the great advantage in the heavier weight of shot of his short-range cannons. Perry's advantage in firepower was partially countered by the fact that most of his big guns were short-range carronades, measured by the weight of the iron shot they fired. Capable of inflicting much greater damage, thirty-two-pound carronades had to be within about two hundred yards in order to be effective.

In command of the *Lawrence*, Perry ordered a final meal for all crews, along with a double shot of grog (whiskey mixed with water). As was customary before naval battles, sand was strewn about the deck to give the men better footing once the blood began to flow.

Perry then ordered his battle flag hoisted. Sewn by a group of Erie women, the flag was emblazoned with the famous defiant declaration, "DON'T GIVE UP THE SHIP." These had been the last words of Perry's good friend Capt. James Lawrence, killed earlier that year in another naval battle, and after whom Perry's flagship was named. Finally, at about 11:45 A.M., the first shot was fired by the British long-range guns. A light breeze hampered Perry's ability to close within carronade range, and so for the first forty-five minutes of the battle, the *Lawrence* took a bloody beating.

For reasons never fully explained, and over which historians have continued to quarrel, Master Commandant Jesse D. Elliott, of the other large brig, *Niagara*, kept his vessel back for the entire first phase of the battle. Elliott had distinguished himself in earlier naval actions and obviously was no coward. Some historians believe that Elliott may have felt stung when Perry was given command of the squadron when he had been expect-

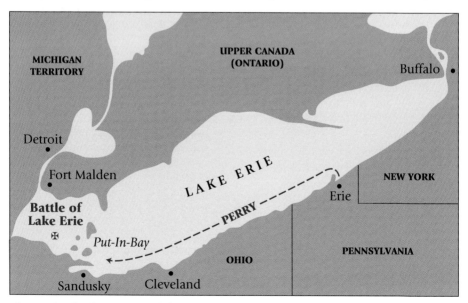

The Battle of Lake Erie. *Perry's fleet sailed from Erie in early August and engaged the British on September 10, northwest of Put-in-Bay.*

14

*The **Rallying Cry** on the battle flag had been the last words of Capt. James Lawrence, a comrade of Perry's who had been mortally wounded on the USS* Chesapeake, *off the Boston harbor in June. A British crew from the HMS* Shannon, *which had just collided with the American ship, jumped aboard and opened fire.* U.S. NAVAL ACADEMY MUSEUM

ing that opportunity. In addition, Perry's order had been for the vessels to stay in a compact formation and in line and to keep close to the *Lawrence*. The *Caledonia*, the smaller vessel between *Niagara* and *Lawrence*, proved very slow moving. Elliott also insisted afterward that the wind was dead and thus he could not sail any faster—though his having only set partial sail weakens this defense. Moreover, Perry advocates in this historical debate have long insisted that once Elliott saw *Lawrence* taking such heavy fire from three British vessels, that should have overridden the previous order and compelled him to move forward.

At any rate, what ensued aboard *Lawrence* for the first two and a half hours of the battle was horrific carnage. Starting with a crew of 102 men, as nearly a third of the ship's crew was too ill to report for duty that morning, Perry saw 22 of his men killed and 66 wounded—a casualty rate exceeding almost any battle throughout the Age of Fighting Sail. And with the fleet's two surgeons down with lake fever the morning of the battle, medical care of the wounded and dying fell to the young surgeon's mate, Usher Parsons.

In the parlance of the day, Parsons was "reading for medicine." With the wounded being carried below deck at a furious pace, all Parsons could do for most men was tie up bleeding arteries and attach a few splints to shattered limbs. Five cannonballs ripped through the ship's heavy timbers into Parsons's makeshift hospital in the officers' wardroom. Parsons had just placed splints on one man's broken arms when a ball tore off the man's legs. Only when a leg or arm hung by a shred did Parsons amputate that afternoon. However, in the forty-eight hours following the battle Parsons operated on ninety-six men, American and British, performing numerous amputations. Quite astonishingly, only two of the men died. That record of medical success in battle was

The Transfer. In 1873, William Henry Powell (1823–1879) commemorated the most dramatic moment of the battle—Perry's transfer from the battered Lawrence *to the* Niagara, *amidst heavy fire—in his painting* The Battle of Lake Erie. U.S. SENATE COLLECTION

not exceeded in American military history until the Korean War. He later attributed his achievement to having had to delay the amputations because of the heavy burden of wounded until the men were out of shock, and to the fresh lake water and air.

Incredibly, Perry remained uninjured. At about 2:20, he spied the undamaged *Niagara*, turned over command of the *Lawrence* to Lieutenant Yarnall, and with four of his remaining crew, rowed back to *Niagara*. Placing Elliott in charge of the gunboats, Perry assumed command of *Niagara*. With a quickening breeze at his back, Perry ordered more sails set and moved swiftly toward the British. Although the *Lawrence* had taken a beating, Perry's crew had been able to inflict severe blows on both the *Queen Charlotte* and *Detroit*. Many guns had been dismounted or otherwise rendered useless; much of the rigging had been shot away;

all of the senior officers were either killed or injured. And so, with *Niagara* now upon them, the British were unable to maneuver their undamaged sides to face *Niagara*. Indeed, as they tried to do so, *Queen Charlotte* and *Detroit* collided, and their rigging became entangled. Perry ordered a port broadside fired at the schooners ahead of the *Queen Charlotte* and *Detroit* and a starboard broadside to rake the large vessels. With a fresh crew and ship, victory for the Americans was swift. Within fifteen minutes, what had looked like certain disaster turned into a stunning victory. After returning to the *Lawrence* to receive Barclay's surrender, Perry penned his famous message to Gen. William Henry Harrison:

We have met the enemy and they are ours: Two ships, two Brigs, one Schooner, & One Sloop.

PERRY LUCK

Commodore Oliver Hazard Perry was a man of extraordinary ambition, courage, and seafaring skill. He also carried an uncanny streak of good luck right through the battle. Here are a few examples:

- The British never attacked the shipyard, thinking that Perry had it too well defended, when, in fact, they probably could have done so successfully. Barclay sailed from Presque Isle at the end of July, giving Perry just the time he needed for the cameling operation.

- Every officer aboard *Lawrence* was either killed or wounded except Perry and his thirteen-year-old brother. At various points, men right beside Perry, to whom he was giving orders, moments later were severely wounded or killed.

- Perry's favorite black spaniel ran about the deck until he was confined to a china closet in the berth deck below, where he howled throughout the battle. The china cabinet was hit by a cannonball, but the dog escaped.

- After two hours of battle, one of *Lawrence*'s boats was still afloat, being towed astern. It had a hole shot through it, but the hole was above the waterline. During the passage to *Niagara*, the British continued to fire at the small boat and yet did not hit their target. Perry's survival that afternoon may well have been aided by his having worn a plain blue sailor's coat rather than his formal—more noticeable—officer's attire.

- The wind freshened as Perry assumed command of *Niagara*, just when he needed it most.

Perry's luck finally did run out, however. In 1819, while en route to Trinidad following a diplomatic mission to Venezuela, Perry contracted yellow fever and died on his thirty-fourth birthday.

No nation had ever before been able to defeat and capture an entire squadron of British ships. This upstart American fleet, built in the middle of a ferocious Erie winter on the edge of the frontier, out of materials hauled from hundreds of miles away, became the first to accomplish the feat. It was also the first time the U.S. Navy had fought and won a fleet action—moving, firing ships against enemy vessels doing the same.

THE AFTERMATH

Occurring at a particularly difficult time during the course of the war, the Battle of Lake Erie restored national morale and confidence. Strategically, it left the United States in command of Lake Erie and forced the British to evacuate Detroit. In the weeks after the battle, Perry ferried General Harrison's troops across Lake Erie and helped the future president intercept and defeat retreating British troops and their Indian allies at the Battle of the Thames River (Moraviantown). It was at this battle that Tecumseh perished and, with him, any remaining hopes of maintaining his fragile Indian confederacy. The British never regained a measure of strength in the Old Northwest, and Native Americans never again—east of the Mississippi—put forward such a determined, intertribal effort to stop westward expansion of the Americans.

In sum, *Niagara* played a decisive role in winning the pivotal Battle of Lake Erie, which firmly secured what was then the northwestern boundary of the United States. A battle that probably should have been handily won but was nearly lost was salvaged dramatically through the valor, perseverance, and good fortune of O. H. Perry.

The War of 1812 ground on for another fifteen months. Indeed, the

The Final Stage of the Battle. *Safely aboard the undamaged* Niagara, *Perry gained the upper hand and reversed the course of the battle, bringing a decisive victory for the Americans.*
PENNSYLVANIA HISTORICAL AND MUSEUM COMMISSION

results of the Battle of Lake Erie are more sharply defined than the ironic and rather ambiguous end of the war itself. The Treaty of Ghent, signed December 24, 1814, officially ending the war, reestablished conditions between the United States and Great Britain as they had existed before the war. Expansionist Americans had to surrender the goal of taking Canada and in that sense lost the war. Impressment did not end, nor was trade with European markets revitalized by the end of the war; British defeat of Napoleon did that. Some matters were more clearly determined: The eastern Canadian-American border was firmly set. Canadians, having repulsed several invasions of their country, saw in the War of 1812 a defining, nationalizing moment. Americans were turned away from their attempted Canadian conquest. Defeat of the Indian-British

alliance, however, fully opened the door to westward expansion. The real losers in the War of 1812, therefore, were the Native American tribes, whose last major unified stand against white expansion east of the Mississippi River came to a tragic end.

THE USS *MICHIGAN/WOLVERINE*

Erie's important role in the early history of the U.S. Navy extended through most of the nineteenth century, triggered largely by the continuation of tense relations between the United States and Great Britain following the War of 1812. The Rush-Bagot Agreement of 1817 between the two nations attempted to demilitarize the boundary by placing limitations on the level of naval armament allowed each side. It was, however, largely a truce of convenience. For the next several decades, both sides violated its terms when political or military events and economic conditions seemed to warrant. Most notably, in 1837, an uprising of independence-minded Canadian citizens received military and political support from Americans across the border. Several skirmishes resulted in the death of one would-be revolutionary and in a British decision to rearm Canada with naval warships to protect Ontario. This flagrant violation of the 1817 agreement, along with a subsequent border incident in Maine and the brazen patrolling of the U.S. shores by armed Royal Navy steamers, in turn triggered a U.S. response. Passage in 1841 of the Fortification Act authorized funds for construction and arming of naval steamers on the northwestern Great Lakes. The particular concern was the defense of Lake Erie, and late that year, Navy Secretary Abel P. Upshur ordered construction of one steamer for that purpose.

Upshur had no ordinary wooden steamer in mind. Rather, this was to be the first iron-hulled, steam-driven warship in the U.S. Navy. Decades before, the British had conceived methods for iron ship design and construction. Commercial contractors in the United States had been experimenting with such technology since the 1820s, and Upshur believed that the new technology could be made to work for the navy. In addition, recent innovations in anthracite coal smelting and the existence of vast amounts of coal made it economically advantageous for the United States. Built in Pittsburgh by the firm of Stackhouse and Tomlinson in 1842, transported to Erie via canal, and reassembled in Erie in 1843, the new ship was christened the USS *Michigan*, after the twenty-sixth state, and was launched on December 5, 1843, in Erie.

The *Michigan* was a steam-powered paddle frigate brigantine with a deck length of 167 feet and a beam, or hull width, of 27 feet. A medium-size warship, the *Michigan* was fast, sleek, and menacing in appearance. Clocked at more than thirteen knots when its boilers were only working under one-half to two-thirds capacity, the ship traveled faster than any naval or commercial vessel on the lakes before it. Outfitted with auxiliary brigantine rigging as well, the *Michigan* was capable of being powered by sail but rarely was. To fulfill its purpose, the ship was armed initially with two sixty-four-pound guns and four thirty-two-pound carronades. The ship's armament changed throughout her lifetime, however, depending on the circumstances.

USS Michigan, *the first iron-hulled warship in the U.S. Navy, was built to put a check on British naval strength in the Great Lakes, but was instead employed to quell civil disturbances and assist distressed ships.*

LAKE SUPERIOR MARITIME VISITOR CENTER, DULUTH, MINNESOTA

REEDER COLLECTION, THE MARINERS' MUSEUM, NEWPORT NEWS, VIRGINIA

The Crew of the **Michigan** *in the 1860s.*

Since the USS *Michigan/Wolverine* was stationed in Erie throughout her nearly eighty years of service, she became a significant part of the social fabric of the community. Scores of Erie men were drawn to the ranks of the U.S. Navy, in part, at least, because of the ship's presence. Seven of those men became admirals—more than from any other city in the United States. Quite a social life developed around the ship, particularly in the winter layover season. Erie girls dreamed of receiving invitations to parties held aboard ship. So many officers and crewmen of the *Michigan* married young Erie women that the city acquired the nickname, "Mother-in-Law of the Navy."

No blood was ever spilled on the decks of the *Michigan*, though her mission of patrolling the western Great Lakes did draw her commanders and crew into numerous contentious and often violent conflicts. Built as a strategic counterthreat to British naval strength on the lakes, the *Michigan* ironically became embroiled in thirty years of mostly American civil disturbances. Among these was the Wisconsin and Michigan timber rebellion of the 1850s, in which the *Michigan* was called upon to protect federal lands from egregious timber pirating. Less honorably, the ship's commander and officers played rather shadowy and ignoble roles in Michigan's Beaver-Mackinac War, which resulted in the assassination in 1856 of a Mormon religious leader. Then, in the summer of 1863, the *Michigan* and her crew were called to Buffalo to help quell Civil War draft riots. Just after the war, the armed presence of the *Michigan* played a central role in suppressing strikes in the copper mines of the upper Michigan peninsula. Finally, the ship aided in putting down the 1866 attempted armed invasion of Canada by Irish-American patriots who called themselves Fenians. The Fenian movement sought to foment an insurrection in Ireland to bring about the end of

British rule through a convoluted, often bizarre political and military strategy that involved entrenching themselves on British-Canadian soil and drawing the United States and Great Britain into armed conflict. This final episode was linked to the occasionally strained U.S.–British relations that had prompted construction of the ship in the first place.

When not on the lakes troubleshooting political and civil conflicts, the *Michigan* often came to the rescue of distressed vessels. In this way the ship is connected with Lake Erie's voluminous and tragic history of shipwrecks. In an area of central Lake Erie often referred to as the Lake Erie Quadrangle, situated between Presque Isle and Long Point, Ontario, 429 vessels have gone down— more than in any other place in the world. And from 1844 until 1903, the USS *Michigan* became involved in more than fifty such incidents in an effort to save crew, passengers, and often the ship itself.

The USS *Michigan* served sixty-one years of active naval duty. In 1905, with the commissioning of a dreadnought battleship named *Michigan*, the iron gunboat's name was changed to *Wolverine*. With changes in technology and U.S. military priorities, the *Wolverine*'s days were numbered. It was officially decommissioned in 1912 and placed on loan to the Pennsylvania naval militia, for whom she served as a training ship for the next eleven years. In 1913 Lt. Comdr. William Morrison of the *Wolverine* led the effort to raise *Niagara* from her watery grave in Misery Bay and restore the ship. It was the *Wolverine* that towed the reconstructed *Niagara* around the Great Lakes during the grand centennial celebration of the Battle of Lake Erie. A decade later, on August 15, 1923, the ship's engines suffered their first breakdown in nearly eighty years of service

The Port of Erie at its maritime zenith.

when a connecting rod snapped three feet from the port engine's crankshaft. It proved to be the fatal blow. The ship was taken out of service completely, and for the next twenty-six years, various entities shifted the responsibility for restoring or scrapping the vessel as its weathered hull lay deteriorating in Presque Isle Bay. Although saved from the World War II metal recycling crusade by no less than President Franklin D. Roosevelt, the historic ship tragically met the scrap heap in 1949—one of the greatly mourned events of Erie local history.

FISHING CAPITAL OF THE WORLD

Erie's maritime heritage is not restricted to its naval history. The civilian and commercial maritime history of Erie is centered on a rich tradition of fishing and shipbuilding. Native American legend held that the long, narrow spit of sand, named Presque Isle by the French, was created by the Great Spirit as a protective arm offering refuge to fishermen being chased by one of Lake Erie's notorious sudden and ferocious storms. This Indian belief is folkloric evidence that white settlers were not the first to enjoy Lake Erie's rich bounty of fish. Erie's great fishing industry, however, did not begin until after the first fishing steam tugboat was launched in 1881. Within two decades, there were nearly 100 such

Fish Tug, Circa 1902. Rocket *was the first metal tug in Erie. At the time, more than 100 commercial tugs were fishing Lake Erie.*

vessels trawling the waters of Presque Isle Bay and Lake Erie, and by 1923, a record 144 commercial fish tugs operated out of the city. The men who worked the fish tug fleet hauled in, by the ton, Lake Erie whitefish, pickerel, pike, and perch. Packed in ice in railroad boxcars, the fish were shipped to cities throughout the East and Midwest. Also flourishing on Erie's bayfront at the turn of the century were ten commercial fish-processing houses, two large icehouses, three major boat- and shipbuilders, three ship chandlers, and a sailmaker near the East Basin. Dozens of restaurants, hotels, and boardinghouses served the fishing fleet. The zenith of the regional fishing industry was between 1910 and 1930, when Erie was regarded as the freshwater fishing capital of the world.

In addition to the steam tugs that came to dominate the bayfront, Erie has a great shipbuilding tradition. In the 1840s, for example, Erie's Charles Reed built and acquired a fleet of side-wheeler steamships so large that he became known as the "Steamboat King" of North America. In the 1860s, Capt. W. W. Loomis became Erie's first noted shipbuilding craftsman. A builder of fish tugs and steamships, Loomis is most noted for his design of what became known as the "Erie boat," a shallow-

draft, skeg-built, inboard-ruddered fishing vessel that was powered entirely by sail. Erie boats, each of which Loomis tested personally before handing them over to the owner, featured masts of equal height and sails of equal shape and square footage to ensure greater speed and maneuverability. They became a favorite of fishermen because their large netting could stow a great volume of fish.

Loomis was followed by master boatbuilders like Harold Paasch, Herman Lund, and James W. Nolan. From the early decades of the twentieth century through the 1980s, their boatyards built and serviced hundreds of fish tugs, sailboats, and excursion and party boats. These were craftsmen in the true sense of the word, each of them combining the science and art of shipbuilding in such unique ways that their work became internationally known. Among Nolan's boats, for example, were three excursion vessels built for Philippine president Ferdinand Marcos.

Many of the ethnic peoples who came to Erie were drawn here by the lake trades and maritime industries. Fishermen, stevedores, sailors, carpenters, ship-

Erie Boat, 1897. The famous boats constructed by W. W. Loomis were powered by sail and could store large quantities of fish.

Maritime Workers. The workforce of Erie's maritime trades in the early twentieth century included strong representation from recent immigrant groups. ERIE MARITIME MUSEUM

wrights, and laborers on Erie's bayfront counted among their ranks great numbers of Portuguese, German, Irish, Russian, Swedish, Finnish, Polish, Italian, and African Americans. Each group had its own neighborhood, centered around the church and social hall, many of which are still thriving, including the Russian Old Believer church, with its onion-shaped domes, on the bluff overlooking the Maritime Museum. At the turn of the last century, many of the ethnic groups built and clustered themselves in boathouse enclaves on the waterfront. A few remnants of the boathouse era are visible from the Bayfront Highway.

From 1920 to 1990, Erie's commercial fishing industry slowly but steadily passed into history, primarily the victim of a combination of overfishing and pollution. Around 1900, whitefish became the first species to suffer serious decline and eventual extinction, followed by herring in the 1920s. The legendary, almost prehistoric-looking Lake Erie sturgeon, some of which weighed in at more than 250 pounds and stretched to six or seven feet in length, disappeared by the 1950s. Most catastrophic was the sudden demise of the great blue pike.

Sports fishermen as late as the 1940s caught hundreds of blue pike in a single outing. And then in 1958 came the devastating news that they were gone. Many observers blamed the apparent extinction of blue pike and the demise of other species on the rising levels of pollution in the lake. Industrial, agricultural, and residential pollution in the Great Lakes region had increased to such a point that by the late 1960s, biologists grimly announced "the death of Lake Erie." Compounding the misery for commercial fishermen was increased competition from sportsfishermen, which, along with larger forces, such as the growth of supermarkets and mass fish processing, signaled the death of commercial fishing in Erie. One by one, commercial fishermen surrendered the business, leaving by the turn of the next century a single lone fisherman to carry on the tradition. Although the vitality of the lake recovered to a great extent by the year 2000, it was too late for extensive commercial fishing. Sport and recreational fishing, however, remain strong components of the regional tourist economy and help maintain the link to Erie's great fishing past.

Niagara
Reborn in the Twentieth Century

W hen the War of 1812 ended, the *Niagara* returned to Erie, where she served as station ship for the next several years. The battered *Lawrence* had been repaired and used as a hospital ship for the wounded during the winter of 1813–14. The ship served briefly in the 1814 campaign on Lake Huron and was then returned to Erie.

With the Rush-Bagot Agreement of 1817 between the United States and Great Britain, the Great Lakes were demilitarized. Thus in 1820 both the *Niagara* and *Lawrence* were deliberately scuttled in Misery Bay, across the Presque Isle harbor from the village of Erie, near the site of the Perry Monument. Built hurriedly as they were with substantial amounts of untreated green timber, both ships had suffered fairly severe wood rot in the few years before they were sunk.

In 1875, with the approach of the American centennial celebration, the *Lawrence* was raised and taken to Philadelphia to be displayed as part of the event. While awaiting exhibition, however, Perry's original flagship burned in a warehouse fire in 1876.

THE CENTENNIAL *NIAGARA*, 1913

Niagara continued to lie in her watery grave for another thirty-five years, receiving the benefit of Misery Bay's cold waters, which preserved her remains better than if she had been lying aground. In 1908, however, planning began for the centennial celebration of the Battle of Lake Erie, which brought the first of several reconstructions of Perry's victorious relief flagship. Among the commemorative actions taken were the establishment of a centennial commission; the Pennsylvania legislature's appropriation to assist in the construction of the Perry Memorial at Put-in-Bay, Ohio, near the site of the battle; and the raising and reconstruction of *Niagara*.

Ownership of the vessel's deteriorated hulk, at the time still in the hands of Daniel Dobbins's grandchildren, was transferred to a centennial commission. Fund raising commenced in 1911 and Lt. Comdr. William Morrison of the USS *Wolverine* was charged with directing the project to raise the vessel. Diver surveys of *Niagara* declared the ship worthy of restoration, and in March 1913, local shipbuilder William Paasch began the operation. The hulk was freed from its

Niagara *in* 1913. ERIE MARITIME MUSEUM

The Hulk of Niagara *was raised from Misery Bay in 1913 for the first of several restorations.* ERIE MARITIME MUSEUM

nial occasion. Erie shipbuilders Hansen and Lund rebuilt the hull of the ship, though they were able to salvage only about 10 percent of the original ship in the reconstruction. Without original ship's plans to work from—and it is unlikely they ever existed—Hansen and Lund primarily used the remains of the ship to guide their work. By June, she was ready for launching, final rigging, and outfitting. Masts, spars, sails, and guns were all produced by local Erie firms. Receiving her first visitors on July 2, 1913, *Niagara* was grandly celebrated in Erie during the designated Perry Week of July 6–12.

sandy, muddy encasement, and then workers brought *Niagara* to the surface with the use of four chains—one forward, one aft, and two amidships. Once towed across the ice to her reconstruction site at Crystal Point on Presque Isle, the first rebuild of *Niagara* commenced in April 1913.

Just as a century before, but without the ominous threat of battle, work went forward hurriedly that spring and summer to prepare the ship for the centen-

Under tow of the USS *Wolverine*, a historic ship in her own right, on July 13 the ship departed on a two-month voyage around the Great Lakes. Lieutenant Commander Morrison directed a crew of twelve men aboard *Niagara*, as well as the forty-six men of his own ship. From mid-July to mid-September, the ships traveled to ports throughout the Great Lakes, from Buffalo, New York, to Green

Centennial Celebration. Patriotic crowds boarded the restored Niagara *in 1913 to celebrate the 100th anniversary of the battle.* ERIE MARITIME MUSEUM

Niagara *on Tour.* USS Wolverine, *formerly* Michigan, *towed* Niagara *to ports in the Great Lakes during the centennial celebration.* ERIE COUNTY HISTORICAL SOCIETY & MUSEUMS, ERIE, PENNSYLVANIA

Bay, Wisconsin, to Put-in-Bay, Ohio, for a grandly patriotic September 10 centennial celebration of the Battle of Lake Erie. Enthusiastic crowds greeted the ship in every port she visited. Throughout the 1913 voyage, *Niagara* apparently sailed under her own power only once, and her replica guns were never fired. Her mission that summer was purely to inspire patriotic pomp.

In the wake of the successful 1913 centenary, a large question loomed: Who would be responsible for maintaining the ship? That proved a daunting challenge to both the citizens of Erie and the commonwealth of Pennsylvania for the next seventy years. The state had assumed ownership of the vessel following the dissolution of the centennial commission. In 1917 the Pennsylvania legislature transferred ownership of the brig *Niagara* from the commonwealth to the city of Erie. In the empowering legislation, the state authorized the city to do

with the ship whatever it deemed proper for its preservation, including transferring ownership to another municipality or once again scuttling the ship.

BUILDING THE THIRD *NIAGARA*, 1928–63

Scuttling the ship may have been a more prudent course, for it remained docked in the bay's West Basin for fifteen years

Niagara *in the early twentieth century.*
ERIE MARITIME MUSEUM

Niagara, 1963. In the fifties, the ship was placed in a concrete cradle to give it support.
ERIE MARITIME MUSEUM

before any substantive action was taken to care for the vessel. In 1928, the USS Niagara Association was formed for the purpose of acquiring and restoring the ship and making it the centerpiece of a museum at the foot of State Street. By this time, the ship was sinking at her mooring and had become a danger to fishing docks around her and to the visiting public. In 1929, the city of Erie transferred ownership to the Niagara Association and worked with the organization to retrieve the ship from her berth and place it on a wooden cradle. Major fund-raising efforts commenced that year, but with the onset of the Great Depression and organizational difficulties, they sputtered along unsuccessfully.

Within two years, the state had once again claimed ownership, establishing the Flagship Niagara Commission and committing $50,000 for the brig's restoration. So in 1931, the second reconstruction of *Niagara* began, with local shipbuilder Herman Lund charged with the work of totally rebuilding the rotting vessel. All manner of fund raising was attempted during the leanest years of the Depression to try and sustain the rebuilding of the ship, including the sale of pieces of the salvaged, but unusable,

Niagara that had been held by the Erie County Historical Society.

Unfortunately, by 1938—the year of the 125th anniversary of the Battle of Lake Erie—the hard economic realities of the era forced the state to shut off the little economic support it had continued to provide to the project. At that point, the Niagara Commission had $8 in the bank. The state soon renewed and strengthened its commitment, however.

In 1939, the legislature transferred formal custody and responsibility for restoration and maintenance from the Niagara Commission to the Pennsylvania Historical Commission (later PHMC), with the former body remaining in an advisory capacity. That year, $10,000 was appropriated to sustain the effort. In 1940, President Franklin D. Roosevelt, a former assistant secretary of the navy, approved a $30,000 request to have *Niagara* become a federal Works Progress Administration (WPA) project. This second reconstructed ship differed from the 1913 version. The Historical Commission contracted with Howard I. Chapelle, a noted marine architect of historical ships, to design plans based on more accurate knowledge of ships built elsewhere during the period by Noah Brown. By 1943, the hull was completed and the third U.S. Brig *Niagara* was launched that October. It lacked masts, spars, and sails; the finishing rigging and outfitting would have to wait.

And wait. For a variety of reasons, including questions regarding the location of the restored ship, shortfalls in state funding, and continued deterioration of the rebuilt hull, the rigging was greatly delayed. In 1951, the rotting hulk was placed in a concrete cradle on State Street while it waited further state action. Shipbuilder Herman Lund found in 1956 "advanced rot in every one of the ship's timbers without exception." He recommended that the state halt its incremental and protracted effort to refurbish the ship and instead initiate once more a complete reconstruction of *Niagara*.

For the next few years, numerous proposals as to what to do about the ship surfaced in Erie and at the Pennsylvania Historical and Museum Commission (PHMC), including scrapping the ship and building a museum featuring a model of *Niagara* and the remaining keel. But with the 150th anniversary of the Battle of Lake Erie approaching, big ideas would have to wait. Sufficient state appropriations arrived in time to refurbish the ship to a degree presentable for public visitation. *Niagara* was finally rigged, outfitted with cannons, and rededicated in a grand 1963 sesquicentennial celebration.

But the late 1960s and 1970s again saw public neglect and ship decay. Although *Niagara* was entered on the National Register of Historic Places in 1973, and despite various sporadic and valiant efforts by historians, public officials, and local businessmen, in the early 1980s the *Niagara* still lay at the foot of State Street in its concrete cradle. It appeared more like a grave.

NIAGARA SAILS AGAIN, 1990–

And then, when all appeared lost, the PHMC worked in concert with a group of Erie citizens to breathe new and lasting life into the historic ship. In 1981, the Flagship Niagara League was formed by citizens of northwestern Pennsylvania who slowly but steadily committed themselves to the idea of reconstructing the ship, not as an outdoor museum piece, but as a working ship that would sail.

Niagara League and PHMC officials were inspired by successful efforts around the country to reconstruct accurate replicas of historically significant ships and also received encouragement and advice from the Maritime Office of the National Trust for Historic Preservation. With support from the city of Erie, the parties by 1982 committed themselves to the central goal of a newly reconstructed *Niagara* and a host museum that together would become the centerpiece of a revitalized Erie waterfront. Late that year, the league was officially incorporated as the local non-profit associate group of the PHMC that would channel local fund-raising and volunteer efforts toward that objective.

While the location and design of a museum home for the ship seemed unsure for the next several years, one thing was clear: The reconstruction of a sailing *Niagara* would go forward with one million dollars authorized in 1984 by the legislature. In 1986, the PHMC chose Melbourne Smith, a respected designer of contemporary and historic sailing vessels, to lead the reconstruction of the new *Niagara*. At that point, public visitation to the crumbling old hulk on State Street was closed, as Smith prepared to dismantle it. He hoped to

Dismantling Niagara. *By 1987, the ship was in such a state of decay that it was destroyed. A few timbers were saved for the reconstruction of a new ship.*

Reconstructing **Niagara.** *In 1988, construction of the new ship began.*

ERIE MARITIME MUSEUM

salvage as many historic timbers from the ship as possible and incorporate them into the new vessel.

In 1987, the PHMC engaged the Pennsylvania Conservation Corps (PCC), a state-level, modern-day version of the New Deal–era CCC program, to reconstruct the *Niagara.* Funds and labor provided by men and women employed by the PCC were crucial in the rebuilding of the ship and, later on, in its maintenance. In late summer that year, demoli-

tion of the old *Niagara* was complete. Although most of the vessel was found to be severely dry-rotted, more than one hundred original timbers were preserved and treated for long-term conservation. Eventually, shipbuilders installed some of these in various nonstructural portions of the hull—precious few, but enough to carry the 1813 spirit of the ship.

Replaying the scene from the winter of 1813, materials for the reconstruction of *Niagara* began arriving in Erie in the winter and spring of 1988. On May 7, the keel for the new vessel was laid at a bayfront construction site just west of State Street. Construction of the hull of the ship went forward expeditiously.

On September 10, 1988, in ceremonies marking the 175th anniversary of the Battle of Lake Erie, the hull was launched at the bayfront wharf of Erie Sand and Gravel. Lifted by a large crane from a wheeled dolly, the *Niagara* was gently placed in Presque Isle Bay. Several thousand people attended the event,

Flagship of Pennsylvania. The ship received this official designation by the Pennsylvania legislature in 1990. A month before, Niagara's *sea trials were held.* ERIE MARITIME MUSEUM

NIAGARA'S SAILING CREW

Although the 1813 crew of *Niagara* boasted 155 men, most of them served on gun crews. With twenty guns aboard, keeping the armament firing absorbed most of the crew in battle. That was the essential purpose of any warship: to serve as a floating platform for artillery to engage and destroy that of the enemy. Today's *Niagara*, however, sails with a crew of approximately 40 men and women, up to 19 of whom are paid professional sailors who work on vessels of varying size and type, some of which sail all over the world. Some have stayed with *Niagara* from one season to the next; others leave and then return years later.

ERIE MARITIME MUSEUM

ERIE MARITIME MUSEUM

Niagara has had professional crew from the Marshall Islands and from all over the United States. Volunteers, who fill out the ranks of the crew, come from all over, though the majority are residents of northwestern Pennsylvania. Whatever their origin, they learn the ropes the old fashioned way—by training from seasoned crew and officers. Seasoned mariners, both paid and volunteer, teach the green hands everything: hauling lines, tying the correct knot, furling and stowing sail, maintaining the rigging, and handling the ship's three boats. Crew members must learn everything from the ancient nautical language of a sea-man to modern navigational skills and emergency procedures. Since late 1991, the crew has been led by Capt. Walter Rybka, who has been sailing and working on various kinds of ships for all of his adult life. Prior to coming to *Niagara*, Captain Rybka led the restoration of the merchant vessel *Elissa*, now berthed in Galveston, Texas.

Extensive work goes on in the winter months, as five or six of the professional crew members and as many of the local volunteers as can be mustered do the required maintenance work to keep the ship sailing in perpetuity.

NIAGARA'S SHIP'S COMPANY AND LIVING-HISTORY PROGRAM

Organized in 1984, the Ship's Company is a group of volunteer naval enthusiasts associated with the Flagship Niagara League who regularly conduct living-history programs and demonstrations at Erie Maritime Museum and, when the ship's schedule permits, aboard *Niagara*. Meticulous about their research and period clothing, Ship's Company volunteers take great pride in their presentation of histori-cally accurate and dramatic programs for the public. They frequently travel to other War of 1812 sites and throughout the Erie community. Related to the company is the museum's first-person interpretive program. Generally on weekends and for special events, volunteer interpreters portray a number of well-researched historic characters from the War of 1812, USS *Michigan,* and fishing eras.

COMMONWEALTH MEDIA SERVICES

including Gov. Robert Casey and naval and maritime history enthusiasts from the East Coast.

By spring 1990, the final stage of the project began. On June 5, the main- and foremasts were stepped in a brief ceremony. Following ancient maritime tradition, officials embedded coins—an 1810 silver dollar and three 1990 dollars—in the fore- and mainmast steps. Masts and sails followed shortly thereafter. On July 18, 1990, *Niagara's* sea trials were held and one month later, the brig *Niagara* was officially commissioned "Flagship of Pennsylvania." An act of the state legislature designated Erie the ship's home port and mandated that her new life would not be as a stationary museum piece. Rather, this ship was to have an active sailing program, serving as a "goodwill ambassador" for Pennsylvania. On voyages to the Great Lakes and along the Atlantic Coast, *Niagara* would not only educate visitors about the Battle of Lake Erie and the ancient tradition of square-rig sailing, but also promote visitation to Erie and Pennsylvania's many other historical museums and heritage sites. It was unprecedented: Never before in America had a state committed this level of support to a ship's reconstruction and its long-term future.

THE ERIE MARITIME MUSEUM

While construction of the *Niagara* was completed, plans for a permanent home for the ship had stalled temporarily. A new opportunity for a berthing and museum site arose when, in the late 1980s, the Pennsylvania Electric Company (Penelec, now GPU) opted to shut down its Front Street Station. Since 1917, the facility had been generating electricity and steam heat for the city of Erie through the operation of five coal-fired steam generators. A large mountain of coal occupied the ground just outside the generator building, which would become the Erie Maritime Museum. When they initially decided to close the facility, Penelec officials had determined to demolish the entire complex. After discussions with local officials, however, the company opted to save its turbine building and have it become part of a broader public-private partnership to redevelop Erie's bayfront.

The plan centered around the construction of a new home for the Erie County Public Library, which would adjoin a restored generator building to house the museum. Library director Michelle Ridge provided critical support to the concept before leaving for Harrisburg when her husband, Tom, was elected governor of Pennsylvania in 1992. She and other leaders envisioned a complex similar to the Carnegie Museum and Library in Pittsburgh, only this one would be situated on the pictur-

esque shores of Presque Isle Bay with a stately nineteenth-century square-rig sailing ship berthed beside it.

The Erie architectural firm of Weber Murphy Fox designed and led construction of the new library, which opened its doors in December 1996. Beginning in 1993, rehabilitation and restoration of the adjacent Penelec Front Street Station went forward. Extensive cleaning of the building and modification to heating, cooling, and security systems were just a few of the elements of that process that would take several years to complete.

By the end of 1997 the building was ready to accept the first of its exhibits. By the following spring, exhibit installation was nearly complete, as was the new berth for *Niagara*, excavated on the north side of the library-museum complex, named, in an elementary school

Main Museum Floor of the Erie Maritime Museum. ART BECKER PHOTOGRAPHY

contest, Bayview Commons. The vessel, moored since 1993 at the foot of Holland Street just to the east, occupied its new home in May 1998. The Erie Maritime Museum opened its doors in May 1998 with a grand two-week celebration featuring naval and maritime speakers, musicians, and historical reenactors from the East Coast, Great Lakes, and Canada.

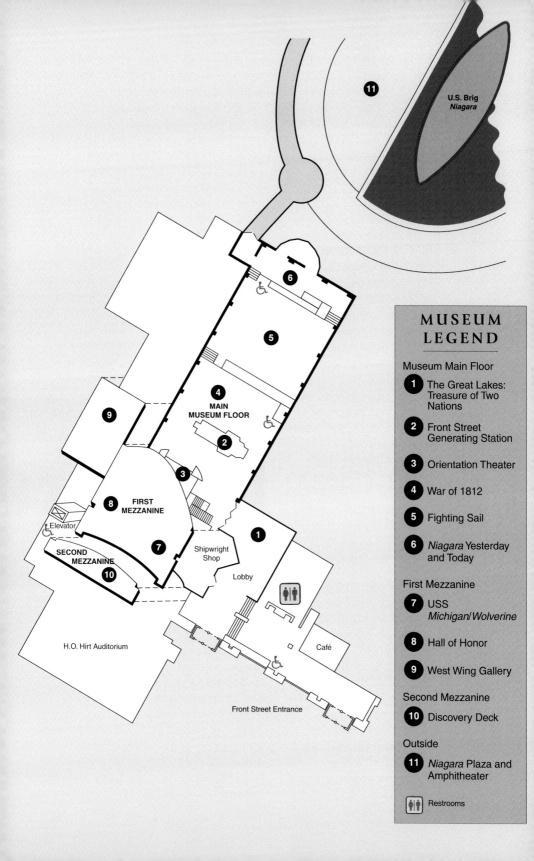

U.S. Brig
Niagara

11

6

5

4

**MAIN
MUSEUM FLOOR**

2

9

3

8 **FIRST
MEZZANINE**

Elevator

7

Shipwright
Shop

1

**SECOND
MEZZANINE**

10

Lobby

H.O. Hirt Auditorium

Café

Front Street Entrance

MUSEUM LEGEND

Museum Main Floor

1 The Great Lakes: Treasure of Two Nations

2 Front Street Generating Station

3 Orientation Theater

4 War of 1812

5 Fighting Sail

6 *Niagara* Yesterday and Today

First Mezzanine

7 USS *Michigan/Wolverine*

8 Hall of Honor

9 West Wing Gallery

Second Mezzanine

10 Discovery Deck

Outside

11 *Niagara* Plaza and Amphitheater

Restrooms

Visiting the Museum and the Ship

KYLE R. WEAVER

1 **THE GREAT LAKES: TREASURE OF TWO NATIONS**

A visit to Erie Maritime Museum begins with the exhibit housed in the museum's main lobby, centered on the human encounter with the environment of the Great Lakes. The "Treasure of Two Nations" exhibit encapsulates in text and striking color photographs the development of the five Great Lakes, the largest repository of fresh water on the planet. After sketching out the distinguishing characteristics of each lake, the display traces the human presence here, from early Native American settlements, to the rise of fishing and logging in the nineteenth century, to the development of major heavy industry and manufacturing in Erie and throughout the Great Lakes basin. Combined with intensive modern agriculture, these became forces for both economic prosperity and ecological degradation. By the 1960s, the burning of the Cuyahoga River in Cleveland and the "death of Lake Erie" caused by eutrophication (unnatural aging) and industrial pollution signified the larger national need for environmental protection. Greater civic awareness and legislative measures indeed arrived in time to restore Lake Erie to a much healthier condition by the 1980s. The exhibit succinctly tells that story.

2 FRONT STREET GENERATING STATION

When GPU made the Front Street Generating facility available for the establishment of the museum, it donated one of the five steam turbine generators that once produced electricity and heat for the city of Erie. Of those five units, three were sold to countries for whom this remains a viable means of energy generation, and one was donated to the Smithsonian Institution in Washington, D.C. Unit 3 remained to help tell the story of the building and Erie's early twentieth-century bayfront. Manufactured by General Electric at its plant in Schenectady, New York, this steam turbine unit, during peak years of operation, produced seventeen thousand kilowatts of power while running at eighteen hundred rpm. Overhead is the Cleveland crane, which once lifted up to fifty tons of generator equipment around the building. It, too, is a reminder of what the facility once was. The crane is still occasionally used to move cannons or other large artifacts in and out of storage. Photographs of the once-sprawling Front Street Generating Station complex help fill out the story of the transformation of this industrial building.

3 ORIENTATION THEATER

The museum's eighteen-minute orientation film, *She Sails*, runs continuously in the seventy-five-seat theater. The film has won or been nominated for several national documentary film awards. It tells the dramatic story of the Battle of Lake Erie and reviews the ship's subsequent reconstructed lives, contemporary crew, and sailing program. *She Sails* prepares visitors well for their museum and ship tour to follow.

4 WAR OF 1812

This exhibit focuses on the causes and major events of America's first "forgotten war." Exhibit text and wonderfully reproduced historical paintings and illustrations chronicle the issues that led the nation to war from the late 1790s through the summer of 1812: the Napoleonic Wars, which triggered Britain's impressment of sailors and the seizure of American ships, as well as the often overlooked issue of American expansionism. These panels impart a sense of how greatly divided the nation was over the decision to go to war. Even those who believed the United States had ample grievances had pause when confronting the reality of war with Great Britain. One part of the exhibit lays out the daunting American challenge statistically: Most striking was the Royal Navy's 740-to-17-ship advantage over the Americans. After considering the issues, museum visitors are given a chance to vote whether they would have chosen war in June 1812 by dropping currency into the "yes" or "no" slots.

The next series of panels takes the visitor through the early phase of the war, mostly grim, for the Americans, lead-

ing to the building and manning of the fleet on Lake Erie in the winter of 1812–13. There are also a case of 1812-era weapons and accoutrements and an electric map providing visitors with a light-up overview of the entire war.

All of this sets the stage for a theatrically composed exhibit of the battle itself, the highlights of which include an original 1887 Julian Davidson painting of the Battle of Lake Erie, glass silhouettes and detailed information on each of the ships in the American and British fleets, reproduced portraits of British and American officers, a reproduction of Oliver Hazard Perry's famous "DON'T GIVE UP THE SHIP" battle flag (the original still hangs in an honored place at the Naval Academy in Annapolis, Maryland), commemorative medals and other artifacts from the battle, and a five-minute film on the Battle of Lake Erie, with theater seating for twenty or more visitors.

5 FIGHTING SAIL

The largest single exhibit of the Erie Maritime Museum, "Fighting Sail" begins with the dramatic *Lawrence* "live-fire" and ship construction display. It is an unprecedented re-creation of the damage inflicted on wooden ships during the Battle of Lake Erie and throughout the Age of Fighting Sail. Using the same kinds and thickness of timbers, in 1997 a Connecticut shipbuilder reconstructed the midship section of *Lawrence*, O. H. Perry's first flagship in the battle. In January 1998, with support from the Pennsylvania National Guard and the U.S. Army, *Niagara* officers, crew, and volunteers transported a portion of the *Lawrence* mockup to a military training site at Fort Indiantown Gap, near Harrisburg. There, using the *Niagara*'s own working guns, ship and military personnel fired twenty-five rounds of 1812-era ordnance at the model from a distance approximating what separated British and American vessels during the first stage of the battle.

What visitors see in this exhibit are the dramatic effects of twelve- and twenty-four-

ART BECKER PHOTOGRAPHY

pound cannonballs, grapeshot and canister shot on the bulwark of a nineteenth-century ship of war. Visitors may initially be surprised to see the relatively mild damage on the bulwark exterior; there are iron fastenings and gun port edges shot away, but in several cases, the cannonballs left near-perfect circles, and a few balls are embedded in the wood planking. It was in the interior, on the ship's main deck, where American gun crews stood trying to return fire, that the power of 350-mile-per-hour cannonballs was most horrifically felt. As visitors walk up a ramp past the exterior of the damaged section, they see a portion of the *Lawrence* left undamaged, then a portion with planking peeled away and timbers revealed, providing a real sense of ship construction and showing the fourteen-inch thickness of timbers and planking the balls had to penetrate. Coming around to the ship's main deck, they see whole sections of the ship having given way in a hail of splinters, some two or three feet long, matching well the accounts of surgeon's mate Usher Parsons, who tended to

ART BECKER PHOTOGRAPHY

the wounded. Making the exhibit more vivid is a diorama of four members of a gun crew, including one African American sailor and one U.S. marine, desperately trying to continue loading their carronade. The exhibit approximates the damage the *Lawrence* would have sustained midway through the two-and-a-half-hour British onslaught, when gun crews would have been reduced from their original seven. A ninety-second video display offers narrated highlights of the 1998 live-fire exercise that created the exhibit.

The balance of the Fighting Sail area simulates portions of a square-rig sailing ship. The undamaged portion of the *Lawrence*, for example, boasts two replica carronades, on which museum interpretive staff, occasionally Ship's Company in period dress, demonstrate the process of loading and firing the guns. Just behind the *Lawrence* diorama is a complete mock-up of the officer's quarters as they appear on *Niagara* and on many ships of the period. Visitors can enter and get a sense of the confined space that housed—and still houses—the ship's officers. A view of the overall cramped conditions is obtained on the exhibit's east wall, upon which is mounted an actual-size cutaway slice of *Niagara*, complete with precise dimensions and diagrammed labeling of main and berth decks, futtocks, knees, and the ship's other key elements. Around the corner is an exhibit on sailors' food and diet.

Dominating this area is the fully rigged and functioning section of *Niagara*'s rig, taken from the ship in its seventh season of operation and installed in the museum in 1997. This fore top gallant—pronounced "t'gallant"—mast, with accompanying fore t'gallant and fore royal yards and sails, reaches to the ceiling of the museum, with lines (ropes) of the rigging extending to the wall and floor. As is the case on the ship, the lines, sails, even parts of the sails each bear distinct names, and in the museum they are labeled. The exhibit gives visitors a glimpse of the bewildering spiderweb of *Niagara*'s nearly two hundred lines when she is fully rigged. When in home port, the ship's crew performs scheduled demonstrations of the rig's operation for training purposes. On occasion, the museum interpretive staff may invite visitors to join in the process of hauling on lines to raise and lower sails. A hands-on knot-tying display completes the exhibit.

 ## NIAGARA YESTERDAY AND TODAY

Situated in a glass picture window at the north end of the museum and overlooking the *Niagara* when she is in port, this exhibit illustrates the post-1813 history of the ship. A rich mix of artifacts, drawings, photographs, and striking video footage enhances this chronicle of the vessel's three twentieth-century incarnations. Among the featured artifacts are a ship spike from the original *Niagara*, a chair and clock fashioned from her timber, and commemorative items from her centennial celebration in 1913. Greatest attention is paid to the 1980s reconstruction. Images of skilled shipwrights and local volunteers working on hull construction reinforce the keen attention to detail and the commitment of Erie people that defined the ship's rebuilding. These images evoke Erie in the winter of 1813, as Perry's fleet was first put together by a combination of locals and skilled shipwrights from the East Coast. Reinforcing that feeling is the exhibit's location overlooking the bay, near the original shipyard where the story began. And where it ended, for within view across the bay in a makeshift hospital on Presque Isle, numerous battle veterans died of a smallpox epidemic during the miserable winter of 1813–14, giving a nearby inlet a name that stuck, Misery Bay; the pond where the men were buried through holes in the ice became known as Graveyard Pond.

7 USS *MICHIGAN / WOLVERINE*

What visitors currently see here—the restored prow, along with the port-side decoratively carved wooden eagle—represents the beginning of what is planned as a much larger exhibit to interpret the USS *Michigan* (later renamed the *Wolverine*), the first iron-hulled warship in the U.S. Navy. Expansion of the exhibit honoring the historic vessel is planned and will feature a wide array of original ship artifacts and photographs, along with a historically correct model of the vessel as she looked in her glory years of the 1860s.

8 HALL OF HONOR

In this area of the mezzanine, colorful banners for each of the fifteen ships, British and American, hang from the ceiling and are attached to monumentlike plaques on the floor that list (to date, for the American ships only) the names of crew members, their positions, and whether or not they were among the casualties.

9 WEST WING GALLERY

With a grand overview of the museum's main floor on one side and Erie's bayfront on the other, this exhibit area holds enormous potential. It currently is occupied solely by the museum's on-site model builder, though plans are under way for the development of exhibits illustrating Erie's broader maritime heritage of fishing, shipbuilding, and shipwrecks.

10 DISCOVERY DECK

Also currently undeveloped, this area is slated to be a hands-on maritime learning center for children of all ages.

11 *NIAGARA* PLAZA AND AMPHITHEATER

Situated between Erie Maritime Museum and Presque Isle Bay—and *Niagara*, when she is in port—*Niagara* Plaza and Amphitheater provides the perfect setting for musical and dramatic performances and lectures on maritime and naval history. With *Niagara* as a picturesque backdrop (or in the case of inclement weather, in the indoor Hirt Auditorium), the museum has featured highly acclaimed American and Canadian folk, maritime, and symphonic music. In addition, the plaza is also the setting for summer living-history events that feature late-eighteenth- and early-nineteenth-century military encampments and artillery demonstrations, domestic arts and crafts, and dramatic first-person interpretations of famous and not-so-famous personages from Erie's naval and maritime history, including Tecumseh, British commander lieutenant Robert Irvin, 1813 Erie women, an 1863 USS *Michigan* sailor, and a 1920-era immigrant fisherman. Such dramatic storytelling brings this history alive for visitors.

U.S. BRIG *NIAGARA*

COMMONWEALTH MEDIA SERVICES

SPECIFICATIONS AND ELEVATIONS OF THE U.S. BRIG *NIAGARA*

Sparred length . . . . 198'	Mast heights	Crew (1813) . . 155 officers and men
Hull length . . . . . . 123' along rail cap	(above load water line)	(present) . . . . . . 42 officers and crew
Hull length. . 110' 8" at load waterline	Foremast. . . . . 113' 4"	. . . . (18 professionals, 24 volunteer)
Max. beam . . . . 32'	Mainmast . . . . 118' 4"	Boats . . . . 2 cutters, 1 gig
Draft at sternpost . . . . 10' 9"	Armament (1813)	Sails . . . . 15 in number;
Displacement . . . . 297 long tons	. . . . . . 18 32-pounder carronades	. . . . 12,665 square feet in area
Tons burthen . . . . 492 $^{60}/_{95}$ tons	. . . . 2 12-pounder long guns	Engines
(old measure)	(present) . 4 32-pounder carronades	. . . . 2 diesel engines, 200-bhp each
Gross tonnage 162	. . . . 2 12-pounder long guns	Propellers
(present-day regulation)		. . . . . 2 featherings, 34" in diameter

DRAWING BY MELBOURNE SMITH,
INTERNATIONAL HISTORICAL WATERCRAFT SOCIETY

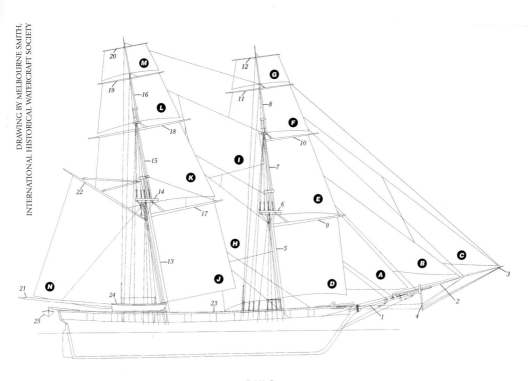

SAILS

A. Fore Topmast Staysail	1. Bowsprit	14. Main Top
B. Jib	2. Jib Boom	15. Main Topmast
C. Flying Jib	3. Flying Jib Boom	16. Main Topgallant Mast
D. Fore Course	4. Martingale	17. Main Yard
E. Fore Topsail	5. Foremast	18. Main Topsail Yard
F. Fore Topgallant	6. Fore Top	19. Main Topgallant Yard
G. Fore Royal	7. Fore Topmast	20. Main Royal Yard
H. Main Topmast Staysail	8. Fore Topgallant Mast	21. Spanker Boom
I. Main Topgallant Staysail	9. Fore Yard	22. Spanker Gaff
J. Main Course	10. Fore Topsail Yard	23. Gun Ports
K. Main Topsail	11. Fore Topgallant Yard	24. Cutter (Port and Starboard)
L. Main Topgallant	12. Fore Royal Yard	25. Gig
M. Main Royal	13. Mainmast	
N. Spanker		
(Main Staysail not shown)		

MATERIALS

Niagara incorporates a few of the original 1813 timbers salvaged from her three reconstructions as a nonstructural symbolic presence. Unlike the original ship, which was built hurriedly, the present ship is constructed largely of properly seasoned and treated wood in order to reduce the rate of decay. Here is a partial list of materials used in the current reconstruction of *Niagara*:

Keel, keelson, and frames . . . . laminated yellow pine
Hull and deck planking . . . . Douglas fir
Masts and yards . . . Douglas fir and laminated yellow pine

Sails . . . . synthetic fiber
Rigging (standing) . steel wire covered with polypropylene
Rigging (running) . . . . Dacron polyester and manila

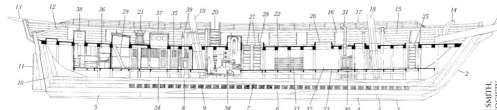

DRAWING BY MELBOURNE SMITH, INTERNATIONAL HISTORICAL WATERCRAFT SOCIETY

ELEVATION

1.	Bowsprit	14.	Cathead
2.	Stem	15.	Bulwarks
3.	Keel Shoe	16.	Gun Ports
4.	Ballast Keel	17.	Hammock Rails
5.	False Keel	18.	Foremast
6.	Keel	19.	Mainmast
7.	Keelson	20.	Gangway Ladder
8.	Rider Keelson	21.	Capstan
9.	Frames ("Floors" across bottom)	22.	Gun Deck
10.	Stern Post	23.	Berthing Deck
11.	Rudder	24.	Bilge
12.	Tiller	25.	Forward Ladder
13.	Gig Davits	26.	Hatch
27.	Main Ladders		
28.	Main Hatch		
29.	After Ladder		
30.	Galley Stove		
31.	Galley Stove Chimney		
32.	Crew Berthing		
33.	Sail Bin		
34.	Engine Room		
35.	Wardroom		
36.	Captain's Cabin		
37.	Wardroom Skylight		
38.	Captain's Cabin Skylight		
39.	Bilge Pump		

ON DECK

Most visitors come away from a visit to *Niagara* impressed by the size of the vessel—masts more than one hundred feet tall, nearly six miles of rope constituting her spider-web rigging, twelve-thousand-plus square feet of sail area. In truth, however, *Niagara* was a relatively small vessel compared to oceangoing ships of the line, and certainly her size shrinks when one considers that 155 men lived and worked aboard her in 1813 (and Perry wanted 170 or more) and that rather than the current complement of six guns, the 1813 ship boasted twenty—ten up and down each side. Among the ship's crew was a contingent of a dozen or so U.S. Marines, who

ERIE MARITIME MUSEUM

were charged with maintaining discipline and order, as well as firing their muskets at the enemy from the *fighting tops* (opposite, top left), platforms that resemble crow's nests, situated nearly halfway up the masts.

Though the ship is no longer engaged in naval warfare, she does sail. Most of the work is accomplished from the deck. A few crew members are needed to go aloft to loose

LOWRY PHOTOGRAPHY

ERIE MARITIME MUSEUM

ERIE MARITIME MUSEUM

sails, untying them from the furled position, but the work of hauling on lines to set sails and trim, or adjust, them to the wind conditions is carried out from on deck. Even with a crew one-quarter the size of the original, space remains at a premium. When not in use, items are stowed out of the way so as to not to interfere with the crew's ability to perform its work. When not in use, *hammocks* are stowed atop the *bulwarks*; in 1813, this had the additional advantage of providing some minimal protection against musket balls and flying splinters. When the ship is under way and sails and lines are fixed in place, the crew will coil and hang the lines on *belaying pins* (top right) in a very orderly fashion. Those pins are located on the *pinrails* along the bulwarks and the *fife rails* at the mast. The fife rails are named for the old practice on naval vessels of stationing a fife player nearby while the crew worked the lines.

Every feature of the vessel has a specific function to perform. Forward on the ship, *Niagara*'s extralong *bowsprit* (bottom right) allowed for greater area of sail and thus increased speed and maneuverability in battle. Also forward is the belfry, which holds the *ship's bell*, used to mark time. *Hatch gratings* are essential to allow ventilation

43

below, where more than twenty men and women (seventy-five or more in 1813) might be sleeping at any one time. *Anchors* were essential in 1813 for avoiding contact with land—a ship's worst enemy, other than an opposing warship. Although less vital today, *Niagara* carries five anchors, ranging in size from twenty pounds to nineteen hundred pounds.

Aft, or rear, on the main deck is the *capstan* (right)—the most powerful piece of manual equipment on the ship. Essentially an immense, human-powered winch, the capstan was needed for weighing anchor, sending masts up and down, moving the ship in and out of docks, and getting cannons aboard. Sometimes a fife player would pipe a tune to keep the crew working in step and help them move the capstan's heavy load. Powered by a dozen crew members pushing the capstan bars, inserted into the sockets, in a circular motion, the capstan is still used for many of these tasks.

Just forward of the capstan are the manually operated *bilge pumps*. All ships leak, through seams and from rain entering through open deck hatches during storms. An essential element of any ship, the pumps are operated periodically by the crew to remove excess water from the ship.

It may be hard to envision, but *Niagara* can be powered by thirty-foot-long oars called *sweeps* (opposite, top and middle), stowed on gallows overhead in the midship area. Even the most well-rested and trained crew working most vigorously would have a difficult time rowing the ship at a speed faster than about two knots. Sweeps were essential, however, for moving the ship under calm conditions in and out of harbors, or to maneuver her so as to bring a broadside to bear on an enemy vessel. The *sweep ports* are small, square holes in the bulwarks between the larger *gun ports*.

The ship's *three small boats* served as the principal link between the vessel and shore, especially in a frontier area like the Great Lakes, which lacked developed ports. The boats performed a number of essential functions: communication, transport of supplies, towing the ship, running anchors out, taking soundings before bringing the ship into a harbor of uncertain depth, carrying raiding or attacking parties ashore, and, in Perry's case, helping to camel and

kedge the ship forward. *Niagara*'s two *cutters* (bottom left) are stowed on the port and starboard sides, with the *yawl* carried at the stern. They are not *lifeboats*, though *Niagara* does carry four of these, of modern form, two stowed forward and two aft.

Niagara is small enough to be steered by a *tiller* (bottom right) rather than a ship's wheel. While there is no definitive information as to what was used in 1813, it is most likely that with nothing more than "plain work" required by

Noah Brown, a tiller—much simpler to make and install than a wheel—would have been the choice. Traditional navigation devices and techniques still guide the helmsman's steerage of the ship, although for the purposes of maintaining the ship's schedule and for the ultimate safety of the crew, modern *navigational equipment* in the form of radar, loran, and radio are part of *Niagara*'s operational equipment—the overriding reason for the engines as well.

45

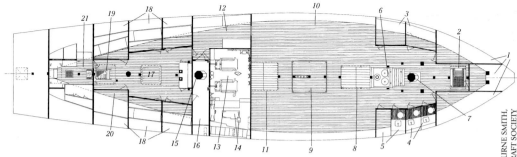

DRAWING BY MELBOURNE SMITH, INTERNATIONAL HISTORICAL WATERCRAFT SOCIETY

BERTHING DECK PLAN

1. Boatswains' and Carpenters' Storerooms
2. Forward Ladder
3. Warrant Officer Cabin
4. Warrant Officer Cabin (Modern Heads)
5. Warrant Officer Cabin (Modern Head and Storeroom)
6. Galley
7. Foremast
8. Forward Hatch
9. Sail Bin
10. Crew Berthing
11. Main Hatch and Ladders
12. Steerage
13. Engine Room
14. Generator
15. Mainmast
16. Magazine Filling Room
17. Wardroom
18. Officer Cabin
19. After Ladder
20. Modern Navigation Station
21. Captain's Cabin

BERTHING DECK

With the space between the main and berthing decks only about five feet, one of the first questions visitors often ask is whether men of 1813 were shorter. The answer is maybe a little, but the cramped berth deck has nothing to do with the size of men and everything to do with Perry's challenge to get *Niagara* out of the shallow channel of Presque Isle Bay. In addition to the cameling operation to kedge the ships forward, the vessels also had to be built shallow-drafted—they could not sink too deeply

into the water—in order to get them over the sandbar at the entrance to the bay. Hence, both large brigs were built with a nine-foot draft. The place to save height was in the berth deck, where men were mostly in their *hammocks*, lashed to rails above and taken down when not in use. The main berthing area was for able-bodied and ordinary seamen. In 1813, the current bathrooms, called heads, located forward on the starboard side, served as *warrant officer cabins*. Extra sails were

stored in the *sail bin* in the center of the berth deck.

Forward in the berth deck is the *galley*, where meals are prepared. Meals in 1813 were simple and crude: salt beef or pork; ship's biscuit, or hard tack; vegetables that could be obtained nearby and that would keep well, mostly peas and potatoes; and the daily noon issue of grog, whiskey and water in the American Navy, often the highlight of the day. It was common for food to spoil and for insects and other vermin to get into the food

46

supply. One of the often-repeated jokes of the era was that it was good that the berth deck was so dimly lit that the men could not see what was crawling around on their plates. Though the food and overall sanitary conditions on the Great Lakes fleet was better than on oceangoing ships, accounts from 1813 indicate considerable complaints about spoiled food. The extensive sickness suffered by Perry's men certainly owed much to these factors. Such as they were, meals were prepared on an *iron galley stove*, or *camboose*, probaby made in Pittsburgh. The current stove, of mid-nineteenth-century design, is temporary until a more historically accurate 1813-era camboose can be made. Men took their meals generally in groups of seven called a *mess*, sometimes the same seven who served together on a gun crew, with one man in the group taking a turn each day of the week for galley duty. They ate on deck on an oiled *mess cloth*.

Further aft of the main berthing area, through the midshipmen's bunk area, is today's *engine room*, near where the *magazine filling room* would have been located in 1813. This is where black powder was poured into flannel cartridges, to be carried to the main deck guns and carronades by twelve-year-old "powder monkeys." All extra supplies, including food, cannonballs, black powder, and repair parts, were carried in the *hold* below the berthing deck, approximately eighteen to twenty inches in depth on either side of the ship and twenty-eight to thirty-two inches in the center. Small holes in the deck planking allowed it to be removed in pieces, providing access to the hold. Additional storerooms for the carpenter, gunner and boatswain's tools and spare parts were located forward in the berth deck.

Aft of the magazine filling room is the *officers' wardroom*, firmly known in 1813 as "officers' country." This area of the ship—main and berth decks—was strictly off limits to ordinary seamen without official

ship's business to conduct. This area of the *Lawrence* was most noted during the Battle of Lake Erie for having served as the surgeon's "cockpit," or operating room. *Officers' cabins* are found on either side of the central dining area—luxurious accommodations with ample personal storage space, compared with that of the ordinary seaman's hammock and seabag. Farthest aft on the ship, and the area accorded the greatest degree of privacy and respect, is the *captain's cabin*.

For information on hours, tours, programs, and activities at Erie Maritime Museum and U.S. Brig *Niagara*, visit **www.phmc.state.pa.us**.

Further Reading

Altoff, Gerard T. *Amongst My Best Men: African American Sailors in the War of 1812*. Put-in-Bay, Oh.: Perry Group, 1996.

———. *Deep Water Sailors, Shallow Water Soldiers: Manning the U.S. Fleet on Lake Erie, 1813*. Put-in-Bay, Oh.: Perry Group, 1993.

———. *Oliver Hazard Perry and the Battle of Lake Erie*. Put-in-Bay, Oh.: Perry Group, 1990.

Altoff, Gerard T., and David Skaggs. *A Signal Victory: The Lake Erie Campaign, 1812–1813*. Annapolis, Md.: Naval Institute Press, 1997.

Ashworth, William. *Lake Erie: An Environmental History*. New York: Random House, 1986.

Berton, Pierre. *Flames Across the Border: The Canadian-American Tragedy, 1813–1814*. Boston: Little, Brown, 1981.

Frew, David, and Dave Stone. *Waters of Repose: The Lake Erie Quadrangle*. Erie, Pa.: Erie County Historical Society, 1986.

Hickey, Donald R. *War of 1812: The Forgotten Conflict*. Chicago: University of Chicago Press, 1989.

Lechner, Carl B. *Erie: Link to the Great Lakes*. Erie, Pa.: Erie County Historical Society, 1994.

MacDonald, Robert J., and Dave Frew. *Home Port Erie: Voices of Silent Images*. Erie, Pa.: Erie County Historical Society, 1996.

Rogers, Bradley A. *Guardian of the Great Lakes: The U.S. Paddle Frigate* Michigan. Ann Arbor: University of Michigan Press, 1996.

Rosenberg, Max. *The Building of Perry's Fleet on Lake Erie, 1812–1813*. Harrisburg, Pa.: Pennsylvania Historical and Museum Commission, 1987.

Rybka, Walter, et al. *U.S. Brig* NIAGARA *Crew Handbook*. Erie, Pa.: Flagship Niagara League, 3d ed., 1994.

Wilbur, C. Keith. *Tall Ships of the World: An Illustrated Encyclopedia*. Chester, Conn.: Globe Pequot Press, 1986.

Books for Children

Berton, Pierre. *The Battle of Lake Erie*. New York: St. Martin's Press, 1996.

———. *The Death of Tecumseh*. Plattsburgh, N.Y.: McClelland and Stewart/Tundra Books, 1996.